Drummond

by Libby Urquhart

Lang**Syne**

PUBLISHING

WRITING *to* REMEMBER

LangSyne

PUBLISHING

WRITING *to* REMEMBER

79 Main Street, Newtongrange,
Midlothian EH22 4NA
Tel: 0131 344 0414   Fax: 0845 075 6085
E-mail: info@lang-syne.co.uk
www.langsyneshop.co.uk

Design by Dorothy Meikle
Printed by Printwell Ltd
© Lang Syne Publishers Ltd 2019

ISBN 978-1-85217-041-7

Drummond

SEPT NAMES INCLUDE:

Begg
Brewer
Cargil
Dock
Doig
Grewar
Gruar
MacCrouther
MacGrewar
MacGrouther
MacGruder
MacGruer
MacGruther
MacRobbie
MacRobie
Mushet
Robbie

Drummond

MOTTO:
Gang Warily.

CREST:
On a crest coronet Or, a goshawk
wings displayed Proper, armed
and bellied Or, jessed Gules.

TERRITORY:
Perthshire.

PLANT BADGE:
Holly or Wild Thyme.

Chapter one:

The origins of the clan system

by Rennie McOwan

The original Scottish clans of the Highlands and the great families of the Lowlands and Borders were gatherings of families, relatives, allies and neighbours for mutual protection against rivals or invaders.

Scotland experienced invasion from the Vikings, the Romans and English armies from the south. The Norman invasion of what is now England also had an influence on land-holding in Scotland. Some of these invaders stayed on and in time became 'Scottish'.

The word clan derives from the Gaelic language term 'clann', meaning children, and it was first used many centuries ago as communities were formed around tribal lands in glens and mountain fastnesses.

The format of clans changed over the centuries, but at its best the chief and his family held the land on behalf of all, like trustees, and the ordinary clansmen and women believed they had a blood relationship with the founder of their clan.

There were two way duties and obligations. An inadequate chief could be deposed and replaced by someone of greater ability.

Clan people had an immense pride in race. Their relationship with the chief was like adult children to a father and they had a real dignity.

The concept of clanship is very old and a more feudal notion of authority gradually crept in.

Pictland, for instance, was divided into seven principalities ruled by feudal leaders who were the strongest and most charismatic leaders of their particular groups.

By the sixth century the 'British' kingdoms of Strathclyde, Lothian and Celtic Dalriada (Argyll) had emerged and Scotland, as one nation, began to take shape in the time of King Kenneth MacAlpin.

Some chiefs claimed descent from

ancient kings which may not have been accurate in every case.

By the twelfth and thirteenth centuries the clans and families were more strongly brought under the central control of Scottish monarchs.

Lands were awarded and administered more and more under royal favour, yet the power of the area clan chiefs was still very great.

The long wars to ensure Scotland's independence against the expansionist ideas of English monarchs extended the influence of some clans and reduced the lands of others.

Those who supported Scotland's greatest king, Robert the Bruce, were awarded the territories of the families who had opposed his claim to the Scottish throne.

In the Scottish Borders country – the notorious Debatable Lands – the great families built up a ferocious reputation for providing warlike men accustomed to raiding into England and occasionally fighting one another.

Chiefs had the power to dispense justice and to confiscate lands and clan warfare produced a society where martial virtues – courage, hardiness, tenacity – were greatly admired.

Gradually the relationship between the clans and the Crown became strained as Scottish monarchs became more orientated to life in the Lowlands and, on occasion, towards England.

The Highland clans spoke a different language, Gaelic, whereas the language of Lowland Scotland and the court was Scots and in more modern times, English.

Highlanders dressed differently, had different customs, and their wild mountain land sometimes seemed almost foreign to people living in the Lowlands.

It must be emphasised that Gaelic culture was very rich and story-telling, poetry, piping, the clarsach (harp) and other music all flourished and were greatly respected.

Highland culture was different from other parts of Scotland but it was not inferior or less sophisticated.

Central Government, whether in London or Edinburgh, sometimes saw the Gaelic clans as

*"The spirit of the clan means much to
thousands of people"*

a challenge to their authority and some sent expeditions into the Highlands and west to crush the power of the Lords of the Isles.

Nevertheless, when the eighteenth century Jacobite Risings came along the cause of the Stuarts was mainly supported by Highland clans.

The word Jacobite comes from the Latin for James – Jacobus. The Jacobites wanted to restore the exiled Stuarts to the throne of Britain.

The monarchies of Scotland and England became one in 1603 when King James VI of Scotland (1st of England) gained the English throne after Queen Elizabeth died.

The Union of Parliaments of Scotland and England, the Treaty of Union, took place in 1707.

Some Highland clans, of course, and Lowland families opposed the Jacobites and supported the incoming Hanoverians.

After the Jacobite cause finally went down at Culloden in 1746 a kind of ethnic cleansing took place. The power of the chiefs was curtailed. Tartan and the pipes were banned in law.

Many emigrated, some because they

wanted to, some because they were evicted by force. In addition, many Highlanders left for the cities of the south to seek work.

Many of the clan lands became home to sheep and deer shooting estates.

But the warlike traditions of the clans and the great Lowland and Border families lived on, with their descendants fighting bravely for freedom in two world wars.

Remember the men from whence you came, says the Gaelic proverb, and to that could be added the role of many heroic women.

The spirit of the clan, of having roots, whether Highland or Lowland, means much to thousands of people.

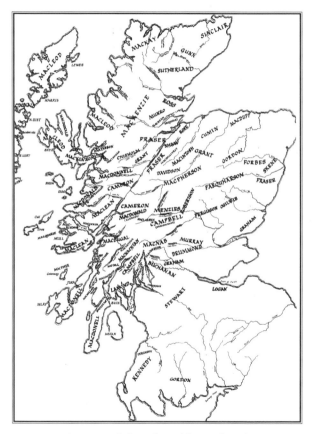

A map of the clans' homelands

Chapter two:

The blood is strong

The history of the Drummond Clan is one of the most romantic and exciting of all of Scotland's great families.

The name is believed to have originated in the 13th century from the lands of Drymen, near Loch Lomond and to the west of Stirling. To this day the chief of the clan, The 18th Earl of Perth, is known as "an Drumanach Mor" or "The Great Man of Drymen".

However the dynasty had a more dramatic beginning in the 11th century when Edgar Atheling (meaning Prince), his mother, two sisters and members of his court fled from England to escape from William the Conqueror after the battle of Hastings. Resigning his briefly declared role as King of England, he secretly set sail for his home in Hungary but was overtaken be a furious storm and ship-wrecked on the coast of Scotland. They came

ashore in the Firh of Forth at a place now called
Saint Margaret's Hope.

In the best tradition of romantic stories,
a handsome and powerful King was waiting at
the rescue. Malcolm III, Malcolm Canmore,
King of Scotland, heard of the plight of the ship
and her passengers and sent messengers to
investigate. They returned with word of "The
stateliness of the older men, the good sense
of the younger, the ripe womanhood of the
matrons and the loveliness of the young girls."
Margaret, the sister of Edward Atheling, was
described as a "matchless beauty". Malcolm
Canmore, who had known her as a child, fell in
love with the woman and then made her his
wife. They were married in the King's town of
Dunfermline and celebrated with great splendour
and magnificence. Margaret and Malcolm had
two daughters and six sons, three of whom
became Kings of Scotland. Queen Margaret of
Scotland died in Edinburgh Castle in 1093
following the news of the deaths of Malcolm
and her son Edward in battle. She was canonised

in 1249 and her body was buried in Dunfermline Abbey in 1250.

Tradition suggests that Maurice, the pilot of the ill fated ship and the youngest son of the King of Hungary, married Margaret's maid-of-honour and that the lands of Drymen were conferred on him. It was from here that the name, Drummond, first evolved. Two theories exist as to the derivation of the name. One is from the Gaelic 'Dromainn' meaning a ridge or high ground. The second derivation is from the Latin 'dromont' – the captain of a swift ship. In those days, when the use of surnames was just beginning, it is not unlikely that Maurice's family would become known as the 'Captains' family.

The first recorded Drummond was the son of 'Malcolm Begg' or Little Malcolm' who was probably named because of his small stature. In 1225, Malcolm was Steward to the Earl of Lennox. Although he did not adopt the surname of Drummond, his younger son Eion of Drummond's tombstone in the ruined church on the romantic island of Inchmahone in the Lake of

Mentieth is inscribed "Johannes de Drvmod filius. Molqalmi de Drvmod".

The grandson of this first Drummond, Sir Malcolm, fought with Robert Bruce at Bannockburn in 1314. He is credited with the strewing of caltrops in pits prepared on the battlefield. The caltrops were vicious four pointed metal spikes which, however they were thrown, would land with one point uppermost. They were concealed in the path of the English cavalry where they pierced the horses hooves when they charged the Scots army. These frightening pieces of ironmongery probably won the day for the Scots and this is why the caltrops form part of the Chief's Coat of Arms and the Drummond motto is "Gang Warily". For his bravery and his part in securing a victory for the Scots, Sir Malcolm was awarded land in Perthshire.

Besides the unpleasant caltrops, a Drummond is also credited with the introduction of the thumbscrews to Scotland. General Sir William Drummond who was later to become the

1st Viscount Strathallan brought the invention back from Smolensk in Muscovy where he had been Governor. Sir William and the notorious Tam Dayell of the Binns used the thumbscrews to agonising effect during their persecution of the Covenanters in 1678.

The Drummonds gained more land in Perthshire in 1345 when the Chief, John Drummond, married an heiress of the Montfichets and became John Drummond of Stobhall. Stobhall is a beautiful mansion in which David Drummond the 17th Earl of Perth lived. John Drummond of Stobhall's sister, Margaret, his daughter, Annabella, were renowned for their beauty and both captured the hearts of kings.

Margaret married King David II the son of Robert Bruce in 1364 and was divorced in 1370. The marriage ended a year before David's death and there were no children.

Annabella Drummond became Queen to Robert III, the second Stewart King. Queen Annabella was a lady of the most exquisite beauty and intelligence. She was celebrated as one of the best Scottish queens and her death in 1401 was regarded as a great loss.

The romantic attachments of the Drummond men, were sometimes less successful. Queen Annabella's eldest brother, Sir Malcolm Drummond of Stobhall was kidnapped by a gang of fierce Highlanders "who maltreated him in prison until he perished".

Sir Malcolm fought with Bruce at Bannockburn

Chapter three:

A royal romance

**Almost a century later a third Drummond lady
became involved in a royal romance and lost
her life as a result. Margaret Drummond, the
eldest daughter of Sir John Drummond, was a
lady of "rare perfection and singular beauty".
She captured the heart of the young King
James IV, and it was rumoured that they had
become secretly engaged.**

Such were the politics of the time that
every possible obstacle was put in their way by
the nobility and the church, both of whom desired
an alliance between James and Margaret Tudor,
the daughter of King Henry VII of England. So
long as Margaret Drummond lived, the Scottish
King would entertain no thoughts of marriage to
another. He was crowned in 1488 and did not
marry until a year after her death in 1501 when he
was nearly 30.

Margaret Drummond's death was deeply

suspicious and it is believed that she was served a poisonous potion with her breakfast. Sadly, the lady was sharing her meal with her twin sisters and her maid and all four of them were killed. One story suggests that the poison was administered at Mass by way of the communion cup.

The sisters were buried together in Dunblane Cathedral in "a curious vault covered in three fair blue marble stanes joined close together." This original tomb has now gone and a brass plaque in the choir is all that remains to commemorate the three sisters and terrible deeds that took place.

James IV's marriage to Margaret Tudor was an alliance of the Thistle and the Rose which later was to lead to the union of the Scottish and English crowns.

The First Lord Drummond acquired the lands of Concraig near Crieff in Strathearn in 1487. He began building a castle at Concraig, that is now called Drummond Castle. This first lord was reputed to be a "peppery old gentleman" and from his bad temper stems the Perthshire prayer "from the ire of the Drummonds, good Lord deliver us." When he was seventy six he was imprisoned for striking the Lord Lyon King of Arms who he thought disrespectful to his grandson, the Red Douglas, second husband of Queen Margaret Tudor. Perhaps one can understand his bad temper when one sees that besides losing his daughter Margaret and her sister, he also lost his youngest son David Drummond who was executed in 1490 for burning a number of their old rivals, the Murrays, in the church at Monzievaird.

The execution of David Drummond

Chapter four:

Murderous times

In 1589, Patrick, 3rd Lord Drummond appointed as his Deputy Royal Forester his kinsman, John Drummond of Drummond-Ernoch. Drummond-Ernoch was hunting in Glenartney when he came upon a band of MacGregors poaching deer, a crime which was often savagely punished. As a punishment to them and a warning to others he had their ears cut off. The MacGregors, who probably held the view that a deer from the hill or a fish from the stream was theirs by right, were enraged by this sight, and in retaliation they returned and murdered Drummond-Ernoch. They cut off his head and concealed it in a plaid.

The horrible trophy was carried along the shores of Lochearn to the home of Drummond-Ernoch's sister, Mrs Stewart of Ardvorlich. The men requested food and in the best traditions of hospitality, she could not refuse them. Mrs

Stewart gave them cheese and bread; she left the room to arrange for other provisions. She returned to find that the severed head of her brother had been placed upon the table, his mouth crammed full with the food. The grisly sight drove the poor woman screaming from the house and she fled to the hills where she remained for several days before her husband found her. The murderers left the house taking the severed head with them. Word was sent to their chief and on the following Sunday the MacGregors all met in Balquhidder Church where a strange ceremony was performed. The Chief walked up to the altar, placed his right hand on the severed head and swore an oath to keep the identity of the murderers a secret and accept joint responsibility for the crime. The clansmen had no alternative but to follow the example of their chief and each of them repeated the same vow.

However, Major Stewart hunted down and captured the MacGregors and had them hanged on an oak tree at Tynereoch between St. Fillans and Comrie. Mrs Stewart who had been pregnant at the time of the outrage, safely delivered a son, who was described as having a "a peculiar temperament" and was said never to have spared a MacGregor.

The MacGregors were hunted down

In 1610 James Drummond, the first Lord Madderty built Innerpeffray Castle. Fifty years later his grandson, the 3rd Lord, established a library in St Mary's Chapel, the burial place of the Drummonds. On this site a new building, Innerpeffray Library, was erected in 1751 by Robert Hay Drummond. It was Scotland's first public lending library and it remained in use until 1968 when it stopped lending books and became a museum and reference library with some 3,000 titles printed before 1800, the earliest dating from 1502. The library is open to the public.

Amongst those volumes is the work of one of the most distinguished members of the clan, William Drummond of Hawthornden. He was descended from the Drummonds of Carnock who were cadets of Stobhall. William studied law in Edinburgh, Bourges and Paris until he inherited Hawthornden in 1610. Here he lived the life of a philosopher and a poet. Although on his death most of his books were left to his old university, some of Sir William's original volumes are still to be seen in Innerpeffray Library.

Chapter five:

The Jacobite cause

During the '15 and the '45, the Jacobite Rebellions, the Drummonds were deeply involved and their territories were a centre of political and military activity. From the earliest times the Drummonds were involved with the royal houses of both Scotland and England, however their fidelity to the Jacobite and the Stuart cause never wavered.

James Drummond, the second Duke of Perth in the Jacobite peerage was one of the first to join the rising of 1715. He was in the thick of the plotting when the Earl of Mar arranged the "Hunting Party" on the Braes of Mar where he gathered around him all those who were loyal to the Jacobite cause. In order to avoid suspicion Mar implied that the meeting was organised for the purpose of a Great Hunt. This was the beginning of the 1715 rebellion, which was to end at the Battle of Sheriffmuir in which Lord

Drummond was described as, "the dashing cavalry commander." He survived the battle and went into exile to join his father at the Jacobite court.

The second Duke died in 1720. The 6th Earl and the 3rd Jacobite Duke of Perth, James Drummond, who had been born in France and remained there to be educated after the death of his father in 1734, returned to Scotland to Drummond Castle to live with his mother. He retained close connections with the Jacobite court and was amongst the first to welcome Bonnie Prince Charlie when he arrived at Glenfinnan in 1745.

Besides the clansmen and adherents, three of the noble family, Lord John Drummond, the Earl of Perth and their cousin, the 4th Viscount Strathallan appeared on the battlefield at Culloden and only one of them was to survive.

James Drummond was acknowledged as an accomplished strategist, and was in command of the Jacobite left flank. He encouraged the demoralised MacDonalds to join the fight. They felt that their position had been usurped by Lord George Murray and his Athollmen on the right flank, a position traditionally held to be theirs since Bannockburn.

"James Drummond, bonnetless, faced them and using all the energy his poor weak constitution allowed, sought to raise morale. They could fight to make this left wing more honourable than the right. If so, he would change his name to MacDonald."

When at last the order came to attack, Lord George Murray and his right wing penetrated the Hanoverian ranks but at a terrible cost. The Duke of Perth appealed to the MacDonalds to follow him across the moor but when they fell in it was to no effect. The disciplined musket fire of the Hanoverians prevented them from finding a home for their swords. Exhausted and with terrible losses they fell back. Weak and in despair the Duke sought to stem the retreat until he too was injured by a bullet in his shoulder.

Viscount Strathallen, who was unhorsed and mortally wounded on the field, was given the last sacrament in whiskey and oatmeal since bread and wine could not be found in time.

After the battle the Duke and his brother Lord John Drummond made the dangerous journey westwards to the sea. Word had arrived that two French ships were waiting at Loch nan Uamh. The journey to the coast took several days and they stayed where they could with friends along the way. These houses in which they rested on the journey were later burned to the ground by government troops hunting for fugitives. Finally they reached the coast where the French warship "Mars" was waiting. This was to be the Duke's last glimpse of Scottish soil for already gravely ill, he died some days later aboard ship and was buried at sea. Lord John Drummond escaped to exile in France.

Such was the respect and affection in which the Duke was held that some years later a private soldier penned the lines:

"O hold me not, dear Mother Earth
But raise me with the Duke of Perth
With many another loyal lad
To wear again the white cocade."

With all the men departed after the battle, it fell on the women left at home to guard the Drummond stronghold. The formidable Duchess of Perth is said to have burned down the keep to prevent it falling into the hands of the Government troops. She was not to be dislodged until 1750.

One account suggests she had also appeared at the battle of Falkirk in 1746, her form changed by the powers of witchcraft. There was a belief that this worthy Jacobite lady made her contribution to the cause by assuming the disguise of a hare for the purpose of spying.

Robert Drummond, Edinburgh printer, was a staunch supporter of the Jacobites. During the occupation of Edinburgh he printed the Prince's manifestos and proclamations. He was later jailed for vilifying the civic authorities, led by his own kinsman, Lord Provost George Drummond.

Chapter six:

The Drummond lands

Until about 1770 the Crieff tryst was the most colourful and notorious throughout Britain.

The town, in the heart of Drummond territory, was a gathering point for the small black cattle from all over the north and west of Scotland with as many as 30,000 of them arriving for sale from as far away as the Outer Hebrides and Caithness. The Earls of Drummond in their role as Stewards of Strathearn held a court to settle disputes, dispense justice and keep order assisted by some of the tenants who held land on the condition that they would assist with the policing of the tryst. The Earl had the power of 'pit and gallow' and the 'kid gallows' of Crieff were reputed to be able to hold twelve men at a time, although the remains of them in Perth museum suggest they may only have held six.

The Drummond Estates were one of the most advanced in terms of improvements and benefited from the efforts of an improving land-lord in the times before the Jacobite Rebellion. The 4th Duke of Perth was a member of the "Honourable Society of Improvers in Knowledge of Agriculture in Scotland", rather than clearing people from the land he was involved in the creation of the "new town" Callander in Mentieth. In the late 17th and early 18th centuries. The Drummonds had introduced Flemish technology and craftsmen into Perthshire which was to dramatically affect the future prosperity of Crieff and Stathearn.

Drummond Castle is now the Scottish seat of the Earls of Ancaster whose family name is Drummond Willoughby d' Eresby.

The Drummond Tartan, also known as Drummond of Perth is believed to have been worn by Bonnie Prince Charlie as a cloak during the Rebellion. It has some of the characteristics of the Royal Stewart tartan.

The Drummond along with the Grant and Fraser tartans were strongly associated with the Jacobite cause.